THE HAYES BOOK OF
MYSTERIES

THE STRANGE, THE BIZARRE, AND THE UNEXPLAINED.

Written by
MARY KAIZER DONEV

Edited by
Nadia Pelowich
Paul Hayes
Curtis Rush

Designed and Illustrated by
RICK ROWDEN

D1087857

Penworthy Publishing Company, 219 North Milwaukee St., Milwaukee, Wisconsin 53202
Printed in Hong Kong

ISBN 0-87617-024-6
Printed in Hong Kong

CONTENTS

PHILADELPHIA EXPERIMENT

It was October of 1943 and the convoy ship named the U.S.S. Eldridge was docked in the Philadelphia harbor. For months scientific teams had hovered about its decks like bees over the making of a nest. But what kind of elaborate nest were they making?

The U.S. Navy volunteers who had signed up for the top-secret experiment were kept in the dark. That it would be a great service to the advancement of technological warfare was all they knew. They had never heard of "Project Invisibility."

But what better way to fool enemy radar? - thought the scientific masterminds - An invisible ship could not be sighted, it could not be sunk and it could roam the waters, creeping up on its victims like an act of God. The enemy would never suspect what hit them.

The cream of the scientific crop was enlisted to bring the idea to reality. They had a theory based on "electrical power fields" and the knowledge of what charging such a field should do; they didn't know for certain that it would work. They had no idea of what would happen if it did. Their tests involving electromagnetism had never been executed on such a grand scale and although they'd developed the most powerful of electromagnetic generators, it was difficult for them to imagine its effect on a ship the size of the *U.S.S. Eldridge*. Finally, after the long months of mental toil, the day had come when the scientists would see what was or was not impossible.

The volunteer crew boarded the ship in good spirits - they were men who rose to a challenge, men who believed that their first duty was to serve their country's needs. Still they knew nothing more than that they were involved in an experiment in military tactics, and in this light, the secrecy surrounding the project did not seem unusual.

With everyone on board and all systems in position, the moment had come. Those who "knew" held their breath as, at last, the switch was flicked.

The *U.S.S. Eldridge* was there...

...And then she was not.

Only a ghostly outline remained as the massive ship vanished in a green fog.

Moments later, to the shock of hundreds of onlookers, she reappeared in Norfolk, Virginia - 250 miles away!

And again, in just moments, she was back in Philadelphia.

The U.S. Navy tried to ignore the many eyewitness reports that poured in. Though labeled "Top-Secret," such an experiment was not easy to hide. Rumors were spread of mass-hallucination but those who had seen it in Norfolk knew differently...yet, they knew only that they'd seen it; they had no explanation.

With time, the *U.S.S. Eldridge* was forgotten, shelved, hidden - but there were some for whom it would remain a nightmare.

One Navy officer, released early from service following the ill effects of a W.W.II "experiment," told his tale.

The crew, he said, had disappeared with the ship. Some passed out and some vanished before his eyes. No one knew what was happening - they never did know what happened. Some saw double and many couldn't think straight after that. Some might be in mental hospitals now.

One man, Dr. Morris Jessup, had collected vast information on the Philadelphia experiment. Having contacted a number of its survivors he was reaching an understanding of what had happened and the chances are good that, were he not killed in 1959 - in an accident - the truth would have come out for all.

But as it is, we may never know. Within the walls of a mental institution an old man could be mumbling about how he disappeared once...once...how a whole ship disappeared. And wouldn't it be nonsense?

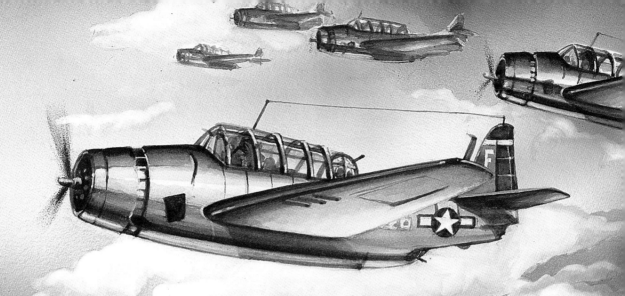

BERMUDA TRIANGLE

For years, the Bermuda Triangle has been famous for a large number of disappearances of boats, people and aircraft which have gone unexplained, or unsatisfactorily explained. The most famous case is that of "Flight 19."

A group of five TBM Avenger fighter bombers left on a U.S. Navy navigational exercise from Fort Lauderdale, Florida, on December 5, 1945 at 2:10 p.m. They were to be gone two hours.

An hour and a half later, Lt. Robert Fox was flying near Fort Lauderdale when he heard a voice on the radio that sounded in trouble. Lt. Fox asked what was wrong; the reply he got was: "This is FT-28. Both my compasses are out, and I'm trying to find Fort Lauderdale, Florida. I'm over land, but it's broken. I don't know how to get to Fort Lauderdale."

Fort Lauderdale control tower confirmed FT-28 to be one of the missing planes, and their instruments showed the planes to be over the Bahamas, almost exactly where they should have been. They could hear the pilots talking, but could not seem to make contact with them. Two rescue planes were sent out to intercept them and lead them home, but 20 minutes later a ship reported seeing one of the planes explode in midair. The second rescue plane arrived at the intercept point and found no sign of Flight 19, and neither did any of the other planes or ships that searched the seas for them in the following weeks. Flight 19 had flown into the heart of the Bermuda Triangle Legend, and taken Rescue Flight 49 with it.

TUTANKHAMEN'S REVENGE

Lord Carnarvon had said he couldn't afford to finance another search. This was Howard Carter's last chance to find the lost tomb of Tutankhamen but the days were coming to an end, they were nearly out of money, and once again - and for the last time - he would have to return to England and to Carnarvon empty handed.

It seemed like he'd been combing the Valley of the Kings for centuries, searching for the lost tomb of the boy king, Tutankhamen. In fact it had been over thirty years. It had to be here! It had to be! - he thought, squinting his eyes against the glare of white sand. And knowing that it was here was the worst of it - because he would not be the one to find it.

On his way to join the others one morning, he was certain his dream had ended, but as he approached the site, the unusual silence told him something had happened.

"What? Could it really be?"

"Yes!" said his headman, running up to greet him. Carter's face flushed with emotion. They had waited so long for this but now, at last, they'd uncovered the first steps into the ground of what might be Tut's tomb.

The expedition dug for five days more before the top of a door and the "necropolis insignia" was discovered and they knew for certain that a tomb lay inside. On November 6, 1922 Lord Carnarvon received the good news in England and quickly packed his bags to join them.

Those last days before the steps and passageway were cleared were the longest, but at last they stood before a thick sealed door which was flanked on either side by two great statues. With slippers of gold on their feet and gold crowns of serpents on their heads, these statues guarded the secrets of thirty centuries. That same evening, as Carter and his party dined at his house, a commotion was heard outside on the verandah. When they rushed out to investigate, they found that Carter's pet canary - a beautiful yellow bird which he'd bought that year to keep him from loneliness - had been attacked by a serpent of a similar kind as those on the golden crowns of the statue-guards. The native staff murmured among themselves that this was just the beginning of the *Pharaoh's curse*. If King Tutankhamen's tomb was invaded, they said, far worse would come to those involved.

Although many valuable articles were found in the first chambers they entered, it was three months before the door to the inner tomb was discovered. It was here, in this last chamber that the King's mummy should lie and with him, according to Egyptian burial traditions, should be the most spectacular of the tomb's treasures. Carter and Carnarvon exchanged a glance. It could still be possible that behind the door would be nothing at all.

Digging carefully at the thick stone of the door, they managed to open a space large enough to enter. Carter led the way, nearly suffocating with the heat wave that rose from the chamber. When they adjusted to the dim light of a single torch, both men wiped their eyes in disbelief. Never in their lives had they seen such valuables! The glimmer of gold was everywhere!

Unlike the other tombs in the Valley of the Kings, which had been looted by ancient grave robbers, Tutankhamen's tomb had never been opened. Since the day the boy king had been brought there to rest and the door sealed - nearly 3,300 years before - no human foot had entered the chamber. The young king's riches, all those things he would need in the next world, lay untouched: statues, weapons, fine vases and jewels, gold carved furniture and animals, feathered fans and a golden throne of the finest craftsmanship, carved with lions' heads and inlaid with gems! But where, they wondered, was King Tut?

Two years would pass before Tutankhamen's coffin was found and opened, but Lord Carnarvon, the man who had financed the thirty-year search, would not live to see that day. A simple mosquito bite acquired on the Tutankhamen site, was to claim his life just five months later. The bite on his face became infected, causing blood poisoning, fevers and swelling. At the exact moment of his death in a Cairo hotel, every light in the city went out and at that very moment in England, at his Hampshire estate, Carnarvon's dog let out a woeful howl - and died.

Later, when doctors would examine King Tut's mummy they would find a small scar on the left cheek of its face, matching exactly the position of Carnarvon's fatal mosquito bite!

Despite the rumors of the Pharaoh's curse, Carter continued his search and on February 12, 1924, the lid of a massive sarcophagus was raised, revealing a wonder no one could have imagined. Inside, a golden coffin carved in the young king's image stared back at them from vacant eyes. From its head protruded a golden snake and on each arm was engraved an open winged hawk. Inside the case...was the king.

Guarding yet more treasures - jewels and gold items - Tutankhamen sparkled beneath their torches. His face masked in an image of tranquillity seemed somehow alive, watchful...aware.

As the most wonderful of archeological finds of the time it seemed well worth the years of waiting; but in the months to come, many of those who had helped to discover the Tutankhamen tomb, would think differently.

It is said that as the men climbed out from their first visit to the inner tomb a native, horror stricken, pointed to the skies. A hawk - ancient Egypt's royal emblem - glided over the tomb and disappeared. Rumors then began among the natives who said it was the boy king's spirit. Angered at being driven from his tomb, they said, King Tut would seek further revenge.

Many believed it was the *Ancient Pharaoh's Curse*, but for whatever reason, the fact remains that in the months and years to come, twenty others connected with the tomb's discovery would die strange and terrible deaths.

Just months after Carnarvon's death, his half-brother died of an abdominal infection and shortly after, Ali Farmy Bey, an Egyptian prince, a supposed descendent of the Pharaohs, was murdered. In just six years there would be a dozen deaths, and by 1935 the total would reach twenty-one. These included Professor Bernadette, director of the Egyptian section of the Louvre, and the American millionaire, George Jay Gould, who caught cold in the tomb and later died of pneumonia.

Only Howard Carter seemed unmarked by the curse and until his own death in 1939 - by natural causes - he publicly scorned the belief of the Pharaoh's curse, thinking it ridiculous.

But if ridiculous, the coincidences are extraordinary, and even as recently as the 1960's two lives were claimed mysteriously.

In 1966 Egypt's Director of Antiquities fought the government's decision to send the Tut treasures to Paris. They should not leave the country, he said, but the authorities disagreed, and the Director, finally giving up, left the meeting. Just moments after he stepped into the street he was hit by a car and killed.

Again, in 1968, a life was claimed when a member of a British radiology team died suddenly following attempts to x-ray the boy king's mummy. They wanted to know how Tutankhamen had died. But perhaps the young king didn't want them to know.

Italian archeologist, Evariste Breccia, believes the curse should not be taken lightly, and that the magic of the Pharaohs is not magic at all but a science - a science we can't understand. Because modern man is used to a certain order to things his mind is closed to other "orders" or ways of thinking.

RADIOACTIVE MUMMIES

Spanish atomic scientist, Luis Bulgarini, said in 1949:

"I believe that the Ancient Egyptians already knew the laws of radioactivity...It is easily possible that they utilized this knowledge to protect their sanctuaries."

He, and others, said that if the ancient Egyptians had spread the walls of their tombs with uranium, the radioactive dust from that uranium could still kill or seriously harm a person thousands of years later. Some believe that mummies themselves are radioactive and that those in contact with them can run into serious problems. This is one reason offered for the sinking of the Titanic.

On April 14, 1912, 1513 people sank to their deaths in the cold Atlantic waters south of Newfoundland. The ship's name was the Titanic - also known as "The Unsinkable."

We know that the ship hit an iceberg and that poorly equipped with too few lifeboats, only a third of her passengers could be saved. What we don't know is why her master, Captain Smith, decided not to take the route he knew, but to alter his course.

Survivors claimed that on that final day, the Captain acted strangely. Following the collision, when serious trouble was apparent, Captain Smith refused aid from other ships and did not, until the last possible moment, instruct his passengers on lifesaving procedures.

Some Egyptologists think that the Captain's "strangeness" was the result of an unregistered passenger. Stored behind the Captain's bridge, on its way to an exhibition of Egyptian antiquities in New York...was an Egyptian mummy!

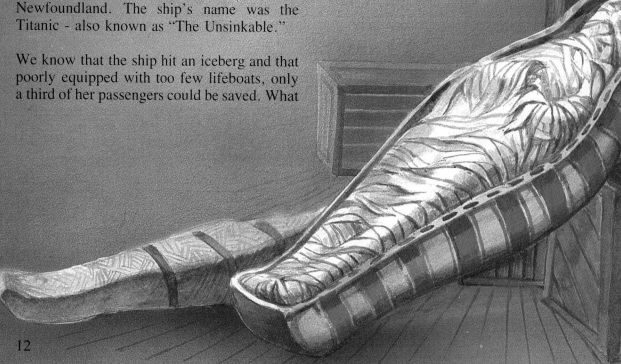

The Titanic Predicted

If it was a mummy that was behind the *Titanic's* sinking it was not the only strange event surrounding this tragedy. There were foretellings of its sad fate in the writings of two authors.

A novel written 14 years before the *Titanic* sank detailed a startlingly similar event. The name of the book was *Futility* and the ship's name, coincidentally, was *Titan*. Created by the author, Morgan Robertson, this fictitious ship was also a luxury liner on her first voyage across the Atlantic. Like the *Titanic*, *Futility's* ship struck an iceberg and suffered great loss of life because of too few lifeboats. The spot in the Atlantic where the fictional *Titan* and the real *Titanic* met their ends was exactly the same.

A short story written 20 years before the tragedy of 1912 not only described the sinking of a *Titanic*-like ship, but predicted that author's own death. W. T. Stead, who wrote the short story, was one of the 1513 who lost their lives when the *Titanic* sank!

OAK ISLAND

Sixteen-year-old Daniel McInness was a good shot. In 1795 small game was plentiful on the south coast of Nova Scotia and Daniel liked nothing better than to try his skills on the surrounding inlets and coves where few ever went. As he paddled toward the small island ahead of him, his gun at his side, he could not have guessed his aim would turn to a hunt for gold. Even less would he have suspected that 200 years later his hunt would continue at the hands of others.

Daniel cached his boat on shore and trundled into the thick oak wood. Perhaps because of his skill with a rifle, he had a good eye and was quick to notice anything unusual. But once he saw it - something hanging from a tree and the huge depression in the ground below - he was amazed that he'd not spotted it sooner. It looked to him like the remnants of an old hoist and the sunken earth below looked like…buried treasure!

"Everyone knows Captain Kidd was in these parts!" he later told his two friends.

The following morning, as the sun rose pink over the lolling waves, the three boys dipped their paddles in the direction of Oak Island. Once there they began digging. They dug until the sweat soaked their shirts and their shoulders ached, until the sun rose high over their heads and fell slowly behind them in the west. Then, as twilight crept into the skies, one of their shovels struck with a dull thud.

In a giddy panic they brushed the dirt aside to find a floor of oak planks. Captain Kidd's treasure lay beneath it, they knew! Pledging silence they returned home, anxious for the dawning of the next day.

In the coming months they would find their days but a repetition of the first. At 10 feet, 20 feet and 30 feet an oak platform stopped their shovels and they grew excited only to find beneath each one…more earth. It was tough work but they were only three people and no one would help them.

"That darn island is haunted," said the mainlanders. "Don't you know there have been strange lights seen on that place before?"

Some even thought it was cursed and that whatever the boys were digging for would come to no good. But it wasn't a fear of ghosts which eventually stopped the three from digging. The summer had long since passed into autumn and jobs had to be found, money had to be made…especially if they were to continue their treasure hunt.

But the shaft went untouched until 1804. Simeon Lynds, a wealthy Nova Scotian, formed the first treasure company. If anyone could get that Oak Island gold, he would, he thought.

After striking eight platforms, three of which were sealed with ship's putty and coconut fibers, a stone was found carved with strange, unclear markings. Beyond this, at a depth of 93 feet they hit something solid. As the daylight was nearly over, Lynds sent his men home. The treasure - and he was sure this was the chest itself! - would wait one more day.

It didn't.

When Lynds and his crew returned the next morning the shaft was filled two thirds with water and no amount of pumping or bailing would lower it. At last, after a final attempt to sink yet another shaft, old Lynds had not a penny to continue.

Daniel McInness had died, but in 1849 his two friends returned to their old site. Although they were now in their seventies, they had never forgotten - the thirst for the treasure had burned a hole in their minds. Before their final attempts caused the base of the shaft to collapse into what they believed was a big cavern, they were mildly rewarded. Once as they pulled their drill from the earth, something was attached to its blade - three pieces of gold chain glimmered temptingly, but it was hardly enough gold to keep the dig going. As they turned their backs to the site, they were almost glad Daniel was already dead - at least he was spared this greatest disappointment.

But others took over where one left off and the search has extended to the present. In the course of those who have tried, nine people have died and the loss in dollars has exceeded $3 million.

The most modern of equipment, bulldozers, drills and mining skills has turned up nothing but a curious respect for the one who designed the money-eating shaft - now known as the "money pit." Created so that it fills with water through the opening of side tunnels, its entry is a problem the best engineers cannot conquer.

Captain Kidd's gold? The crown jewels of France? Ancient South American treasure planted by Spanish looters? There are as many suggestions as to what lies on Oak Island as there are people to wonder about it.

EL DORADO

El Dorado - "the golden place" - has for centuries tempted men into the jungles and mountains of South America. On yellowed maps, faded and frayed, El Dorado's location has never been clear...but it's somewhere...somewhere in the Andes.

Colonel Leonard Clark had a map, a gun, a guide and little more when he set out in June of 1946 to find the golden city. As a former U. S. intelligence officer he had, as well, years of survival training and those years would be his greatest help.

In areas that had never known the feet of white men, and through the worst jungle regions of the Amazon, every imaginable danger awaited. White water rapids, countless diseases, man-eating jaguars, poisonous snakes and spiders as big as a man's fist were just some of them. But perhaps the most frightening was the threat of the natives who were known to cut off people's heads and reduce them to 2 1/2 inches - the Jivaro headhunters!

In his book, *The Rivers Ran East*, Clark tells of his terrible ordeals, experiences that were far worse than his wildest dreams, and in retrospect he wrote:

"...I simply had to find that lost land of treasure, El Dorado, no matter what it had cost others in disappointment and tragedy."

Clark believed he found not one, but six golden cities! At any rate, he did find gold. Others believe the golden city's wealth lies on the bottom of Lake Guatavita, where the Chibcha Indians of Brazil were to have dumped their greatest treasures in sacrifice to their chief. Attempts to drain this lake, however, have been unsuccessful and many have come to think that El Dorado, which means both *golden place* and *golden man*, was a man after all and not a city of riches.

And still, there are those who, like Clark, believe the gold awaits them...somewhere...somewhere in the Andes.

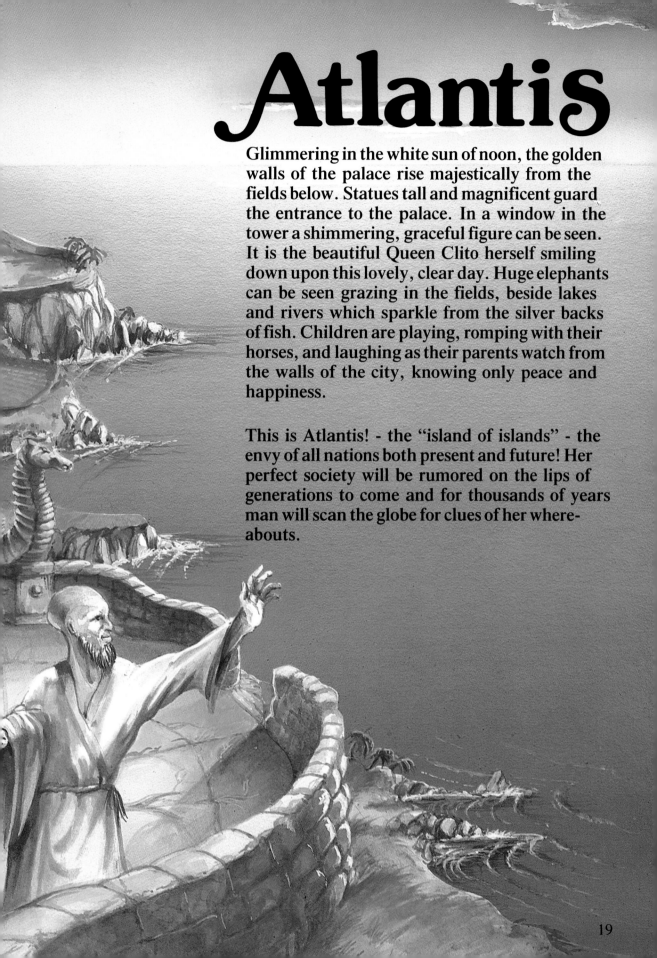

Atlantis

Glimmering in the white sun of noon, the golden walls of the palace rise majestically from the fields below. Statues tall and magnificent guard the entrance to the palace. In a window in the tower a shimmering, graceful figure can be seen. It is the beautiful Queen Clito herself smiling down upon this lovely, clear day. Huge elephants can be seen grazing in the fields, beside lakes and rivers which sparkle from the silver backs of fish. Children are playing, romping with their horses, and laughing as their parents watch from the walls of the city, knowing only peace and happiness.

This is Atlantis! - the "island of islands" - the envy of all nations both present and future! Her perfect society will be rumored on the lips of generations to come and for thousands of years man will scan the globe for clues of her where-abouts.

Ruled by ten kings, the sons of the God Poseidon and his mortal wife Clito, Atlantis is a land known for its just laws. Its citizens fear nothing and there are few who are wrongdoers. Just once, every five or six years, the ten kings gather to pass judgment. A great bull is sacrificed and when the new laws are announced, Atlantis is alive with celebration!

Feasts are spread for all and there is music and game playing. The stadiums are full with the cheering of fans as below on the tracks, the men prepare their horses for the race. Then, with the falling of night, the fine silver temples hum with prayers of thanks, never suspecting that in the hearts of its faithful grows the ugly seed of greed.

As first described by Plato in his books *Timaeus* and *Critias*, written in 355 B C Atlantis grew vain and domineering. Unsatisfied with the boundaries of their paradise the Atlanteans set out with warships to conquer Athens and many of the lands of Europe as far as Italy and Egypt. The gods grew angry and to punish them they caused a volcano to erupt out of the sea and with the fearful force of a resultant "tidal wave," Atlantis was swept into the ocean - without a trace.

For more than 2,000 years man has argued about the Atlantis legend. Perhaps, some believe, the famous Greek philosopher, Plato, just made the whole thing up. Maybe...but in writing the tale Plato did suggest that it was, in fact, an historical - real - event. Other ancient tales, after all have been based on fact. In 1871, German archeologist, Heinrich Schliemann, discovered the legendary city of *Troy* and to the amazement of all the world, the tale of the *Trojan Wars* was found to be based on real places and real people!

Is it any wonder that for hundreds of years, thousands have searched for the lost city of Atlantis? More than 2,000 books have been written on the subject and it has resulted even in a new word being added to the dictionary - "Atlantologist": someone who is an expert on matters involving Atlantis.

Plato said Atlantis lay in the Atlantic, opposite "The Pillars of Hercules" - or, as it is known today, the Straits of Gibraltar. But, opposite the Straits of Gibraltar could mean almost anywhere!

Following the travels of Columbus and his discovery of the new world, a popular theory developed that America was Atlantis, or at least, part of that lost land. How else, they reasoned, could the Aztecs, the Incas, and the Mayans have developed such grand civilizations on their own? Surely, they were survivors, refugees of Atlantis. Even until the 18th century some mapmakers listed America by that name.

Other places which have been suggested and searched as possible sites of the lost continent are Mexico, Central Asia, the Sahara, the West Indies, Spain, Greenland, Newfoundland, and even Britain.

In 1967, a group of perfectly sound and respected scientists announced that they had found Atlantis. Off the Greek island of Crete, buried under centuries-old volcanic ash, a Minoan city was uncovered with traces of canals and harbors such as Plato had described.

It is true the Minoan's collapse has always been a puzzle to historians for they seemed to have all died, suddenly, 3,500 years ago leaving no evidence of their existence after that time. But this particular city discovered in 1967 was by no means similar in size nor wealth to the legendary Atlantis. Only humble dwellings were found and no suggestion of great and beautiful buildings.

So where is Atlantis?

If Plato was just writing fiction, what has everyone been searching for and why? If there never was an Atlantis, why has the idea remained so strong an interest for so many years? The answer might be simple: perfection, the dream of Atlantis or Eden or Utopia has been a common quest of mankind throughout history. Perhaps man is searching for proof that the world could be, or has been, the wonderful place we all hope it might one day be. Then, again, perhaps the dream land of Atlantis really did exist and is waiting beneath the ocean waves to be discovered. Until that day, however, Atlantis will have to remain a mystery.

Nazca Lines

In South America, about 200 miles south of Lima, Peru are the strange markings that have puzzled archeologists of the century. Commonly known as the Nazca Lines, or Inca Roads, they are not roads at all, but lines which connect to make "pictures." But the strange thing about these pictures is that if you were to walk right over them you wouldn't know they were there!

Though science has estimated them to be over 1,500 years old it wasn't until recently, when airplanes began flying over the region, that they were discovered. Before then, people traveling through the area on foot or by horse, had noticed nothing at all because the lines, or pictures, are too big to be seen from the ground. Ranging from several hundred feet to several miles long, to see them in full you must be nearly 1,000 feet in the air.

So what would we see from an airplane window?

Besides large spreading triangles, rectangles and other geometric shapes one can see various designs of people and animals. There is a monkey, a spider, a strange looking hummingbird and a huge whale with a harpoon through its eyes.

What these might mean has many people wondering. Some suggest that they are linked with the positions of stars, that certain lines pointing this way or that, showed their ancient creators how to count the days of passing seasons. Others think they were made as ceremonial walkways and still others believe they were either messages to the gods or even "runways" for ancient aircraft!

As far as we know, the first flight was made in 1903 by the Wright Brothers, so the question is: why, then, did people make pictures so large that they, themselves, couldn't even see them? And how did they manage to carve such perfect images given that they couldn't "see" what they were drawing?

CRYSTAL SKULL

In 1927, in the Central American country of
Belize, an archeological group was digging at the
ancient ruins of a Mayan city, Lubaantun.
Suddenly, a hush silenced the native workers as
one by one they fell to their knees.

An object, like a great jewel, glimmered
strangely in the sun. A crystal skull! As it was
wiped and dusted and the dirt cleaned from its
crevices, the hollow sockets began to glow.

A murmur of prayers broke the silence as the diggers covered their eyes and wept. Swaying with emotion, the 300 native workers bent their heads to the ground covering the earth with their kisses and tears.

Never had the natives seen anything like the object - a beautiful skull wrought of solid crystal quartz, its eye sockets flickering with light - nor had they even heard of such a thing, yet for two weeks after they were unable to work, so affected were they by its image. Anna Mitchell-Hedges, the leader of the expedition, tried to calm them, but nothing she said or did could change their belief that the skull was a "great ancient power."

As ritual objects connected with beliefs of life and death, skulls of clay, wood, bone and shell are common to all Indian civilizations but none of these - which are crude by comparison - look anything at all like the one found at Lubaantun. The Crystal Skull, so finely made and so realistic, seems as though it were made by other hands...but whose? In no known civilization in Central America or elsewhere, has such a relic ever been discovered.

Said to be modeled from the head of a woman, the Crystal Skull becomes a greater puzzle when examined under a microscope. If metal chisels and tools had been used in its making one would see scratch marks - but there aren't any! Its surface is as smooth as glass and so experts think its perfect shape was polished down, little by little, using sand. If this was how it was made, however, scientists say it would have taken 150 years of constant working to complete it.

The mysteries of the Crystal Skull are many and the most curious of these are told by Frank Dorland, an art restorer who spent six years observing it.

Sometimes, he said, the skull would be surrounded by an odd halo of light, and other times it would give off a peculiar odor. As he watched it, images appeared inside - pictures of mountains and faces and fantastic scenes - and on several occasions a high pitch ringing would fill the room where the skull was kept!

Dorland believed the skull had special powers, that it could change people's moods or thoughts. Others believe the power lies in the wild imaginations of those who look at it. And still others think the greatest wonder is that the skull exists at all...who made it, how, and why?

trinket airplanes

Is it a fish, a bird, an insect…or an airplane?

These little gold trinkets from Colombia, judged to be between 750-1,000 years old have, since their discovery, been labeled as "zoomorifica" - meaning, animal-shaped objects. Colombian Indians are known to have made many types of animal-shaped objects in gold and in other metals, and, because of their attention to detail, it is usually easy to tell what kind of animal they are.

Not so, however, with the "little gold airplanes." These trinkets hardly look like either fish or birds and, though they could be abstract designs of an insect, they have a definite "mechanical" appearance. They resemble, most closely, an F-102 Fighter Bomber!

Viewed from all aerodynamic angles - wing shape and position, balance or center of gravity, adequate space for engine, cockpit, sufficient streamlining, elevons, etc. - some aerodynamic engineers believe such objects, on a life-size scale, could surely have flown. Not only could they soar through the air at great speeds, but they would probably have been aircraft far more advanced than any we have now!

If, as the saying goes "anything is possible," then maybe there were airplanes in our skies a thousand years ago. But - it may also be possible that some ancient Colombian Indian got it into his head to make his "insects" differently. If he knew that hundreds of years later his trinkets would cause such arguments, he might have made even stranger things.

SASQUATCH

Louise Baxter of Washougal, Washington was headed home after driving her mother to the airport. The road was deserted and Mrs. Baxter didn't like the odd thumping sound coming from the front end of her car. Suspecting a flat tire, she pulled over to investigate.

While bent, checking the right wheel, she had the uncanny and creepy feeling that she was being watched. She could feel the hairs rising on the back of her neck as she fought the compulsion to turn around. Magnetically, her eyes were drawn to the roadside.

It stood ten feet tall and penetrated her with its stare - a sasquatch!

She screamed, but the creature didn't move. Unaffected by her terror it held its stand as, somehow, in a blind panic, she found her way back into the car.

They go by several names, these famed giants, suspected to be relatives of man. In the Himalayan Mountains they are known as the Yeti or Abominable Snowman, on the west coast mountain regions of North America they are the Sasquatch or Big Foot, and in the Soviet Union they are known as "almas." Many who would never admit to believing in these giants, do, however, believe in the possibilities of their existing. In May of 1978 at the University of British Columbia a most peculiar conference was held - *Sasquatch and Familiar Phenomena* - which served to bring some light on the subject.

Numerous eyewitness accounts and other evidence in the form of footprints, hair samples, tape recordings and photographs, were submitted, but the most extraordinary piece of evidence was the famous *Patterson film*.

It was a crisp fall day in 1967 when Roger Patterson and a friend rode their horses into the mountainous areas of Bluff Creek, U.S.A. With his 16 mm camera strapped to his side, Patterson had hoped to get some footage of sasquatch footprints and scenes of the environment where he believed the creature lived. He never suspected as he galloped round the next bend that he would find the giant "herself."

She was squatted near the river, unaware of their approach. When she turned, calmly, she met them face to face. Neither timid nor excited, she eyed them curiously.

Patterson's horse reared up in terror, flinging him to the ground. His friend raised a gun into position.

"No!" shouted Patterson.

Countless times he'd argued against the shooting of sasquatch, not that he'd ever had the opportunity until now. The only way he would shoot was with his camera and, aiming his lens, he chased the big female who had already begun to retreat into the woods.

The scientists at the University of British Columbia Conference watched Patterson's blurred film skeptically, but then, in the last few frames the picture stabilized and the face of the lumbering giant was enough to make them think twice.

Averaging 7 1/2 feet tall this upright-walking, primate-like creature usually travels alone and usually at night. It has been sighted most often in remote wooded areas and near rivers where it seems they like to bathe.

People camping have known their curious stares and "attacks" which seem intended more to scare than to harm. They've been known to throw things at people but not to hit anyone and though they've chased people it is reportedly in a bluffing way and not with the purpose of catching anyone. Other cases, however, have reported sasquatches as reaching into cars and even chasing them; clocked by speedometers the sasquatch can average a pace of 50 miles per hour!

Grover Krantz and John Napier, the first physical anthropologists to seriously examine the sasquatch phenomenon, say that the "evidence" is remarkably consistent. Napier says the footprints in particular, averaging 17" long, would be nearly impossible to fake as tracks all over North America are so similar.

The best evidence yet of their existence, he believes, is the *Bossburg tracks* - a series of 1,089 prints found near Bossburg, Washington. Made by what was apparently a crippled sasquatch whose right foot was a club foot. To artificially produce such prints would take a vast knowledge of anatomy. There would be too many places for such a hoax to go wrong and in the case of the Bossburg tracks - nothing is out of place, nothing is missing...

...Except the sasquatch who made them.

KOMODO DRAGONS

Sometimes breathing fire, they are the guards of vast treasures, sometimes they are winged flying things which spread good fortune and other times their only purpose is to terrorize and destroy. The dragon, that fantastic reptilian beast, has been known for centuries in nearly every corner of the globe. But why? - from where did people get such an idea?

In 1912 came reports which would shock the world of zoology. Dragons had been found on the small Indonesian island of Komodo!

Though for years fishermen and pearl divers had told tales of giant lizard-like beasts, known on the island to eat pigs and goats, their reports had been dismissed as nonsense. But in 1912, following the report of a pilot who had crash landed on Komodo, an investigation was conducted.

With dogs sniffing at their sides they combed the island, never certain if behind the next bush a dragon would be hiding. If these things, as the natives said, ate pigs and goats, could they not eat a man just as easily?

But their hunt ended successfully. Four of the dragon-like creatures were cornered and captured, the largest of which measured 10 feet in length.

Belonging to an unknown species of giant monitor lizard, they are now known commonly as *Komodo Dragons* - but their mystery does not end in classifying them.

Unknown to the world, the "dragon" had lived for centuries on Komodo. Komodo is a very tiny island. What weird animal forms, we might ask, could exist in areas as vast and impenetrable as the Amazon or African jungles?

Muchalat Harry's Escape

To the Indians of the Nootka tribe of British
Columbia, the sasquatch is a very real thing.
Father Anthony Terhaar thinks so too for he,
like the others, heard the cries of Muchalat Harry
when very late one night in 1928, this brave
Indian hunter returned to camp as terror stricken
as a young child.

A rugged trapper and hunter, Muchalat Harry was known for his fearlessness. No other Indian would venture into the wilds alone, knowing the deep forests as the home of the sasquatch. But Harry was different. Often, and for long periods of time, he would disappear into the thick woods where his favorite hunting grounds awaited him.

On one such occasion Muchalat Harry, loading his gear into his canoe, made off on an extended trapping expedition. A place he knew well, near the Conuma River, was his destination - he would stay there several months.

His trap lines set up, Harry climbed into his lean-to one night beneath a star filled sky. He felt good. Over the months he would collect many pelts which would bring good prices. But, most importantly, the months would be a time of wonderful peace and solitude. As Harry lay, smiling up into the dark night, a heavy footstep nearby made him reach for his gun.

But not soon enough!

Within seconds, before he could realize or believe what was happening, Muchalat Harry was lifted from his bed by a huge hairy arm!

With Harry strapped under its arm, legs dangling, a sasquatch crashed through the dark night woods. Large branches broke easily in its path and Harry, heart beating wildly, was crazed with fear.

After a short distance of two or three miles, they stopped.

The morning dawned on a sasquatch camp. Males, females and young ones crowded round, shy at first, but then they moved closer. Penetrating him with their curious stares, they finally encircled the Indian.

Silence. Muchalat Harry barely breathed.

Strewn about the campsite were many bones, some parched and white, others with the remnants of meat clinging to them. A sickening feeling crept into Harry's stomach. Sitting there in only his long underwear, cold and trembling, the Indian was certain his end was near.

But then, in the afternoon many of the sasquatch disappeared into the woods. Only a few remained at the campsite and their interest in him had shifted to other things. Harry saw his moment - and made his break!

He ran, almost flew through the forest, heedless of the slapping twigs and the stones that cut his feet. Once in his canoe he paddled in a blind frenzy and 45 miles later, on a cold winter night, his screams were heard by his Nootka village.

Father Anthony helped to drag the Indian ashore and it was three weeks before the story was told, so shocked was Harry that he was struck speechless.

Muchalat Harry never ventured into the deep forests again. His gun and all his camping gear, left where they were near the Conuma River, would become the rusting remnants of a once brave man.

THE UNKNOWN SEA

Ancient Norwegian sailors had a name for it - the Kraken. A massive sea beast with enormous eyes and tentacles of up to 100 feet long, it was known to twist its way about the bow of a ship, sometimes sinking it. Sometimes they crawl on board to feast on human flesh. Long thought to be a creature of myth, strange experiences of modern sailors suggest differently - the Kraken, or creatures like it, exist!

In 1973 the *Kuranda*, a 1,450-ton ship was on its way to the Fiji Islands from Australia when violent waters caused it to pitch relentlessly. Banging into the waves with her bow there seemed to be a problem in the ship's balance - it was unusually heavy toward its front.

Suspecting that something had broken loose in the hold, nothing the crew did could re-shift the weight or raise the ship's nose from digging into the sea. At one point the bow dipped so low that the *Kuranda's* whole front was lost in water. She would not come up, but only slowly, little by little did she rise enough for the men to see "something."

"When I got a look at what was hanging on the bow one devil of a shock ran through me!" said an officer.

A massive jellyfish thing clung to the ship's nose, its tentacles sweeping over the deck and curling around the wheelhouse. It was secreting a froth of jelly-like slime, making it impossible to get near.

The lookout man let out a bloodcurdling scream and rolled back onto the deck in pain. Some of the jelly had got onto his flesh, leaving burn marks - in two hours he was dead.

The weight of the creature immobilized the *Kuranda*. With their propeller exposed they could not move ahead and the ship was taking on water at a frightening rate! She would sink, there was no doubt about it, or the monster would get them first.

Keeping back out of reach of the swirling arms, avoiding the slime which spread with every wave, their only hope was to dispatch an S.O.S. If they were lucky, someone would answer.

Nearly a day later, the *Hercules* arrived, the only other ship which had been within their range. With high pressure hoses and steam, the monster - estimated to weigh 20 tons and with tentacles as long as 100 feet - was finally worked loose.

Marine biologists, taking samples from the *Kuranda's* deck, later analyzed it to be a giant species of jellyfish. The Kuranda crew, however, with one man dead and the memory of the horrible thing scarred on their minds, knew it by another name - sea monster.

In 1960 the first descent to the "abysmal depths" was made in a U.S. Navy bathyscaph a submarine-like vessel designed to endure great water pressures. At 35,800 feet in the Marianas Trench of the Pacific, they described the bottom as a "waste of snuff-colored ooze" - and some creatures they observed there had never been known to man.

Such a one is the *coelacanth*. A carnivorous fish measuring about seven feet long and weighing up to 150 pounds, it swam in the earth's waters as long as 300 million years ago. Fossils indicated it had been extinct for about 70 million years. But what was pulled up in the nets of a South African trawler in 1938 was no fossil. Since then, 85 examples of the coelacanth have been found in the Indian Ocean. Scientists believed, as a result, that the possibilities of other prehistoric sea animals having survived, were good.

They were right. Only recently has the ancient relative of the octopus surfaced. Popularly known as the "living fossil" the *Vampromorphes* is a fantastic being with horrendous eyes and luminous colored organs. Science thought it too, was extinct.

Three-quarters of the earth's surface is covered with water; the oceans average 2-1/2 miles deep. Underwater plains cover vast areas. Underwater mountains far higher than Mount Everest break the waves to form islands. There are trenches deeper than deep, reaching 5-6 miles down. And throughout it all are caves — deep, dark, watery hiding places — where species unimagined undoubtedly lurk. Science says that for every five lifeforms on our earth, four of them exist in the oceans, lakes and seas.

Only from what these great waters have chosen to give us - strange sea things washed up on our shores, deposited in our fishing nets or glimpsed above waves - do we have any idea of the vastness of its creations. With exploration and study of some of these things, science is looking at "sea monsters" in a new light.

OGOPOGO

Ogopogo — legend or fact? This is probably the most pondered question in the Okanogan Valley, British Columbia. Lake Okanogan is approximately 130 miles long, from north to south, and is said to be the home of Ogopogo.

Many, many moons ago, the Shushwap Indians first became aware of "Naitaka" (the Lake Monster) who had made its home in Lake Okanogan. As the great monster had a fierce temper when its lake had been invaded by the natives, they soon began to fear and respect the "monster spirit." When the Shushwap needed to cross or bathe in the lake, they brought peace offerings to settle the temper of the giant creature. The Shushwap would throw small animals such as pigs, chickens and dogs into the water in an attempt to protect their own safety when using these quiet but deadly waters.

As time went on, the first pioneers began to settle the area. They too became aware of Naitaka and, like the Indians, they also bore peace offerings for the use of his water. The pioneers soon renamed Naitaka "Ogopogo" (spelled the same backward and forward), and it has never been changed since.

Last seen in 1976 by two fishermen on Lake Okanogan as they were trespassing on the grounds of the "spirit monster," they sighted the well-known body traveling along the waters of the shore until he disappeared. On their return journey they stared in awe and amazement as Ogopogo appeared once again, but only for a few moments.

As quoted by one of the fishermen, "I'm convinced now that there's something in the lake."

Whales and Dolphins

Since man first set a boat into salt waters he has known the friendly company of the dolphin. Swimming alongside and entertaining sailors with fantastic jumps and other acrobatics, the apparently smiling mammal has long been a source of both wonder and fantasy.

The ancient Greeks and Romans believed there was a natural association between man and dolphin and in their observations they were the first to record "dolphin ways" and to try to make sense of them. One thing they noted especially was the above water sounds that dolphins would make in what seemed to the ancients, attempts to speak. The Greeks and Romans believed these airborne cries to be perfectly natural to the dolphin.

They are not.

Dolphins - and their cousin whales - though they have a larynx (or voice box) have no vocal chords and one of the ways they make sounds above water is by emitting air - something which is totally unnatural for them to do.

Then, why do they do it?

Dr. J. C. Lily, famous for his dolphin research, suggested they do it purely for our benefit - so we can hear them. A dolphin or whale's natural sounds are of such a high frequency that it is only quite recently, with special recording devices, that we are able to hear what they sound like in their world - under water. It was then that the beautiful whale songs were discovered, melodies which, sung solo or in chorus, mysteriously change from year to year. These recording devices, and what we can hear as a result, have opened our eyes to a possibility: Do they "talk?"

Dr. Lily believed they could. Not only did he think they spoke to each other by using their high frequency "sonic" language, but he thought that they could be taught to speak English.

In the most unusual of his experiments, a young woman, Margaret Howe, and a dolphin, Peter, lived together in an "apartment" for two and a half months.

With her desk attached to the side of a pool Miss Howe noted the progress of her "roommate." Peter was constantly with her and even at night, as Miss Howe's bed was just inches from the water, Peter would wake her for a game of catch-ball or to join him for a swim. Just one day a week she left him to arrange the tape recordings from their lessons.

Every day would be the same:

"Speak good…speak good boy…Good, Peter, good!" she would urge. And Peter tried. Mimicking as best he could the words she spoke, eventually, he seemed to understand the purpose of the lessons. The greatest day was when he uttered the word "ball."

In the 1960's the leading Swiss scientist, Pilleri, decided the dolphin cerebral cortex — was in every way as developed as that of higher primates. His studies, he said, showed some species of dolphins and especially whales, to have a degree of brain power and brain structure equal to man's. He went so far as to say, "One wonders if they are really animals."

For those who will disagree, there is much to explain about the curiosities of these sea mammals. Jacques Cousteau, among others, has observed them to be unusual for their human-like ways.

When in danger, a dolphin is never deserted but is helped by its entire group. The young especially are watched closely and, when one has wandered astray or near danger, a whack of its parent's tail will keep it in line. When giving birth, a "midwife" stands by to help the newborn surface for its first breath of air, and this midwife or "aunt" will then help with the baby-sitting until the young one has grown.

One of the strangest observations, however, has been of dolphins standing in a circle, their heads together and their tails touching the ocean floor. One wonders what these *conferences* are about - perhaps they are discussing the intelligence of man.

LEVITATION

A slender young man, not unusual in appearance or manner, stands about with many others, chatting and nibbling on dainties from a waiter's tray. The conversation is the type that you hear at parties where people are introduced and pleasantries exchanged. Nothing in the air suggests the miracle that will happen in just moments.

Suddenly, there is a gasp! A hush falls over the crowd as heads turn and eyes widen in disbelief.

The young man, Daniel Douglas Homes, has risen into the air and hovers a foot or more from the floor. He descends and rises yet again...and the third time he rises level with the ceiling!

Described by F.L. Burr, editor of the *Hartford Times*, Homes "palpitated with joy and fear." The young man, then 19 years old, was speechless.

From this first experience in 1852, Homes was to learn control of levitation; he would become over the next forty years, one of the most famous mediums of the 19th century. Demonstrating before such notables as Mark Twain and the emperor Napoleon III, he had so developed his skill of levitating that Homes could perform at will and for the excitement and entertainment of others.

Once, after having gone into a trance, he was reported to float out one window and return through another; the distance between the windows being 7 1/2 feet. He glided into the room feet first and sat down to rejoin his party. These windows through which he left and entered were 70 feet from the ground!

Homes' greatest claim was that his shows were never disproven. Many tried, and failed. Even the great Houdini, master of tricks, could not figure out Homes' secret.

As unusual an experience as it seems, levitation, or claims of levitation, have been with us for thousands of years.

St. Joseph Cupertino, a monk who lived in northern Italy during the 17th century, was known to levitate to the tops of trees when he was very happy. It first happened one day when he was deeply concentrated in prayer. His amazed colleagues believed this to be a sign of holiness but when it began to happen to him often and without warning, he was asked by the other monks to say his prayers alone.

More recent accounts of levitation can be found among the Yogis of East India. A famous instance is the one of Subbayah Pullavar, who in 1936 reportedly floated horizontally in the air for four minutes. Though one of his hands rested lightly on a stick which just barely touched the ground, that the stick was supporting his weight seems unlikely.

Most photographs of levitational experiences are not convincing. The subject seems always to be jumping rather than floating. This is not to say that true levitation cannot be done. There have been so many accounts of the ability in nearly every culture that the possibility cannot be ignored. Controlled scientific experiments, though, have not been able to lift even a feather.

Mahavish Mahesh Yogi, founder of the Transcendental Meditation Movement claims the secret of levitation lies in meditation. In practicing relaxation of both body and mind, a state can be reached where levitation is possible. In a cross-legged position, yogis have been known to rise a foot or more into the air.

There is one thing common to all such experiences of whichever culture or time - the person who is levitating *believes* it is possible. Scientists huddled around a feather do not believe - perhaps that's where the secret lies...in knowing it can be done.

FIREWALKERS

As the moon rises high in the South Pacific, the Fijian natives prepare their dance floor. The pit has been dug 30 feet long, and with the last coals laid, the fire is ignited. As they wait, the sweet scent of roast pig winds around the palms - later, when their heated dance is done, there will be feasting.

A leaf is dropped into the dancing pit to test the temperature. When it explodes on contact, they know it is ready. The drums start and the grass-skirted bodies begin to sway.

One by one, arms waving and flashing grins, the natives dance swiftly over the hot coal bed. The temperatures are nearly 600 degrees Fahrenheit - and they are barefoot.

Firewalking is not confined to the Fiji Islands. As a religious ceremony it is practiced in Tahiti, New Zealand, Malaya, Japan, India, the Balkans, and Spain. To ensure good harvest or purify the soul, in some cultures it is used to prove innocence. If you walk across the coals and your feet burn - you are guilty!

In Fiji, however, it is a ceremony surrounded by laughter and music. The smiling firewalkers seem to feel no pain and though sometimes they are burned, most go unharmed.

That they have callosed feet is one explanation but when examined by doctors their soles are not unusually thick and some are even soft and pliable. Even with calloses they should not survive so well, as the heat is enough to char the leather soles of boots!

Mind over matter - the ability to increase the heat of the body and so master fire - is to most men the power of magic.

Doppleganger

The year was 1944. Griffith, an infantry
sergeant, was cautiously leading his patrol
through an enemy-infested area of France. The
road through the countryside seemed quiet and
serene. Blossoms hung heavily on the trees, and
the only sounds were the buzzing of the insects
and singing of the birds. There was no sign of
the enemy.

Relaxed, the men continued on their way when suddenly, Griffith stopped. On the road ahead of them, a <u>m</u>an in their own uniform waved violently, gesturing for them to turn around. There was something about the man - the way he stood, something about his face…something strangely familiar…horribly familiar. *Go back! Go back!* he seemed to shout, but though his lips moved there was no sound. And then Griffith saw the bandage - the same bandage he'd put on his own face that morning when he'd cut himself shaving - and then he saw the face he knew so well.

The man was Griffith himself!

To the puzzlement of his troop, who couldn't see the apparition, Griffith ordered his men back. Laying low and keeping quiet they wondered what had got into their sergeant - Why stop? Why stop now? - but as they watched an American supply vehicle pass and head down the same road, they were glad they'd remained. In an explosion of machine-gun fire the supply vehicle was destroyed, blown apart before their eyes. It could have been them.

Twenty years later, with France and the war long behind him, Griffith was with his family on a camping trip in Quebec, Canada.

A severe windstorm had struck the area but once it had died down, the clear skies tempted them to go hiking. Tramping through the underbrush they came to a small clearing. It seemed the perfect place to rest, but as Griffith was about to lead his family through into it - there it was! His double!

Though Griffith had aged twenty years, his double had not. It still wore the rumpled sergeant's uniform and still had the bandage on its chin. And once again it waved frantically for them to turn back. Remembering his last meeting with the figure, Griffith obeyed.

As he watched in awe of the image, a huge tree, weakened by the storm, crashed down before his eyes! Under his breath Griffith whispered "thank you" for the second time in his life.

What Griffith had seen both times is a phenomenon known as a "doppleganger," a German word meaning "double-walker." History has produced countless cases of dopplegangers, many experienced by very famous people.

The French writer, Guy de Maupassant was apparently visited by his double in 1885 as he was busy with the writing of his famous horror story *The Horla*. The double appeared one evening, sat down before him and began to recite the very words he was about to write!

Julius Caesar is said to have seen his doppleganger pacing up and down before him, always just before he would have an epileptic seizure. Studies have since shown that people who suffer from certain nervous conditions or diseases - like epilepsy - have a greater chance of seeing their doubles. Stress and fatigue can cause doppelgangers to appear to otherwise normal people.

The OOBE Phenomenon

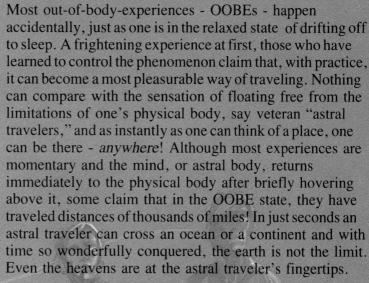

Most out-of-body-experiences - OOBEs - happen accidentally, just as one is in the relaxed state of drifting off to sleep. A frightening experience at first, those who have learned to control the phenomenon claim that, with practice, it can become a most pleasurable way of traveling. Nothing can compare with the sensation of floating free from the limitations of one's physical body, say veteran "astral travelers," and as instantly as one can think of a place, one can be there - *anywhere*! Although most experiences are momentary and the mind, or astral body, returns immediately to the physical body after briefly hovering above it, some claim that in the OOBE state, they have traveled distances of thousands of miles! In just seconds an astral traveler can cross an ocean or a continent and with time so wonderfully conquered, the earth is not the limit. Even the heavens are at the astral traveler's fingertips.

Despite the alleged enjoyment of the out-of-body-experience, most who have experienced the phenomenon are not eager to explore it a second time. Though psychics claim that generally the OOBE is not harmful, it is believed that the possibility does exist that if one has traveled too far, returning to one's body can be difficult. . .and may be impossible.

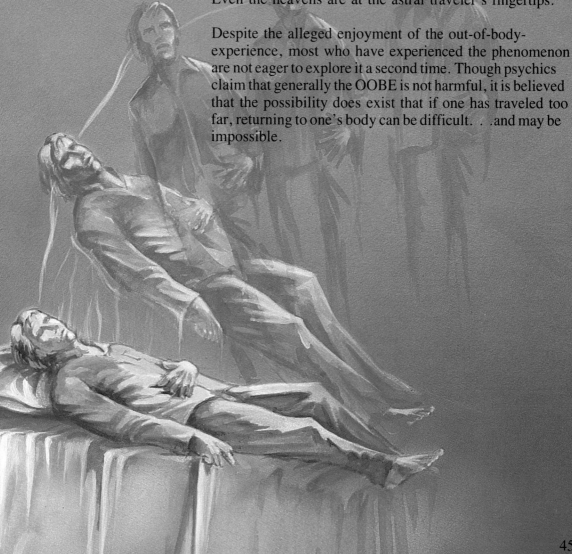

NOSTRADAMUS

In 1940 thousands of "Nostradamus leaflets" fell from the air over France and Belgium. Written on these leaflets were the so-called words of Nostradamus, claiming that Germany would be victor and that France and Belgium would spread conflict.

To oppose these German pamphlets, British Intelligence then spread other Nostradamus predictions: Germany would lose the war, these said.

The words of both pamphlets were lies - war time propaganda to sway the beliefs of the masses.

But who was Nostradamus, in fact? And what did he really say?

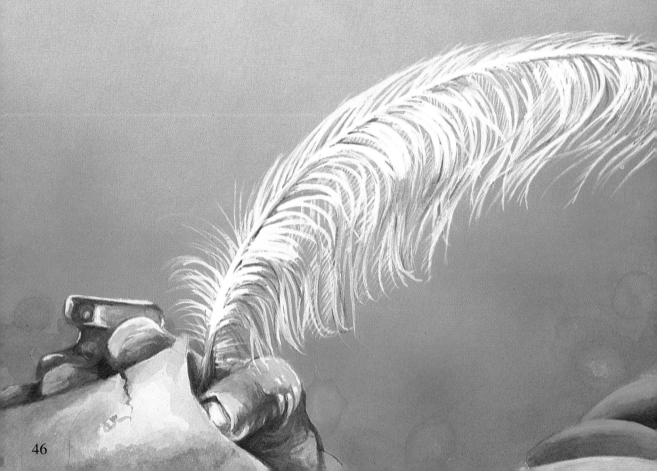

Of Adolf Hitler, German Nazi leader, he apparently said a great deal:

*"In the mountains near the Rhine
There will be born of simple parents
A man who will claim to defend Poland and
Hungary
And whose fate will never be certain.*

*"Beasts wild with hunger will cross the rivers,
The greater part of the battlefield will be
against Hister.
He will drag the leader in a cage of iron,
When the child of Germany observes no law."*

Describing him as a man of great evil, Hitler is mentioned almost by name - *Hister*. But more incredible is the foretelling of the war and that *weapons of the skies and machines of flying fire* would be a part of it.

It is incredible because Nostradamus had never seen an airplane - in his time there were no weapons in the skies - the airplane would not be invented for another 400 years.

He was born in 1503 and became a popular French physician. When a great plague swept the area in 1546 Nostradamus devoted himself to its victims. Though many doctors fled to escape the disease, day after day and long into the nights he worked to save the many who were dying. When the plague had passed, the town awarded him a pension for his courage but Nostradamus had lost something that could not be replaced by money. His wife and two children were among those who had died.

His second marriage to a wealthy widow was to bring a turning point in his career. Besides being greatly devoted to Nostradamus, providing him with a happy family of four children, his new wife encouraged his interests. Her riches gave them plenty to live on and it was not necessary for Nostradamus to work anymore. Giving up the toils of doctoring, he could devote himself to his true love: astrology.

From the many studies and experiments of mind which followed, Nostradamus began writing his "ideas." A book called *Centuries*, written in 1555, is the source of what many people today think are some of the greatest predictions ever made.

The fate of Napoleon, the Great London fire of 1666, World War II, the rise of the Arab empire are just some of the predictions he's credited with. Some translators claim that his writings foretell nuclear explosions, chemical warfare, guided missiles, the invention of aircraft and submarines and the disaster of Hiroshima. In one verse he foretells the rise of the United States as a great world power, saying that *"...it will grow by land and sea to become a face in the east"* - and the twentieth century he describes as follows:

*"The scourge passes, the world shrinks,
There is lasting peace, population increases,
One will travel by air, land, and sea
And wars will begin again and again."*

There are many skeptics, however. Though he sometimes mentions names and places many still find his writings "unclear." He rarely supplies dates for his predictions and because they are often described in poetic-type verse, they can appear like meaningless riddles.

If, indeed, his words are meaningless then we can be thankful, for some of his predictions, according to interpreters, do not paint a bright picture for the future.

*"A great fire will be seen as the sun rises
Noise and light extending far northward
Death and cries are heard within the circle
Death by iron, fire, famine awaiting them."*

The "great fire" some believe to be the beginning of World War III. Let's hope they are wrong.